**Learning Tree
1 2 3**

Where I Live

By Roy Cranley
Illustrated by Bernard Robinson

CHERRYTREE BOOKS

Read this book and see if you can answer the questions.
Ask an adult or an older friend to tell you if your answers
are right or to help you if you find the questions difficult.
Often there is more than one answer to a question.

A Cherrytree Book

Designed and produced by
A S Publishing

First published 1991
by Cherrytree Press Ltd
a subsidiary of
The Chivers Company Ltd
Windsor Bridge Road
Bath, Avon BA2 3AX

Copyright © Cherrytree Press Ltd 1991

British Library Cataloguing in Publication Data
Cranley, Roy
 Where I live.
 1. Geography
 I. Title II. Robinson, Bernard III. Series
 910

ISBN 0-7451-5156-6

Printed and bound in Italy by L.E.G.O. s.p.a., Vicenza

All rights reserved. No part of this publication may be
reproduced, stored in a retrieval system, or transmitted, in
any form, or by any means without the prior permission in
writing of the publisher, nor be otherwise circulated in any
form of binding or cover other than that in which it is
published and without a similar condition including this
condition being imposed on the subsequent purchaser.

I live in a flat in a town.
Lots of people live in the town.
Some of them live in houses.
Some of them live in flats.

The centre of the town is crowded with people.
They work in the shops and offices.
A river flows through the middle of the town.
There are bridges across it.

There is a station in the centre of the town.
On the outskirts there are suburbs.
There are lots of busy roads.
On the edge of town there is an airport.

If you go to the top of a high building, you can see the countryside beyond the town.
You can see the roads and the railway, and the river flowing through the fields.

There are farms in the countryside.
Farmers grow crops in the fields.
Some keep animals too.
They provide the food we eat.

There are not so many people in the country as in the town.
There are not so many buildings.
Most people live in villages or on farms.
Villages are smaller than towns.

People's homes are often miles apart.
Most children have to travel a long way to school.

Beyond the fields, you can see hills and trees.
The trees are part of a forest.
Not many people live on the hills.
It is hard to farm on hilly land.

In the hills the river is narrower than it is in the town.
The river starts in the hills.
It flows downhill very fast.

On the other side of the town, the river is wider and slower.
It flows all the way from the hills to the sea.
On the coast there is another town.

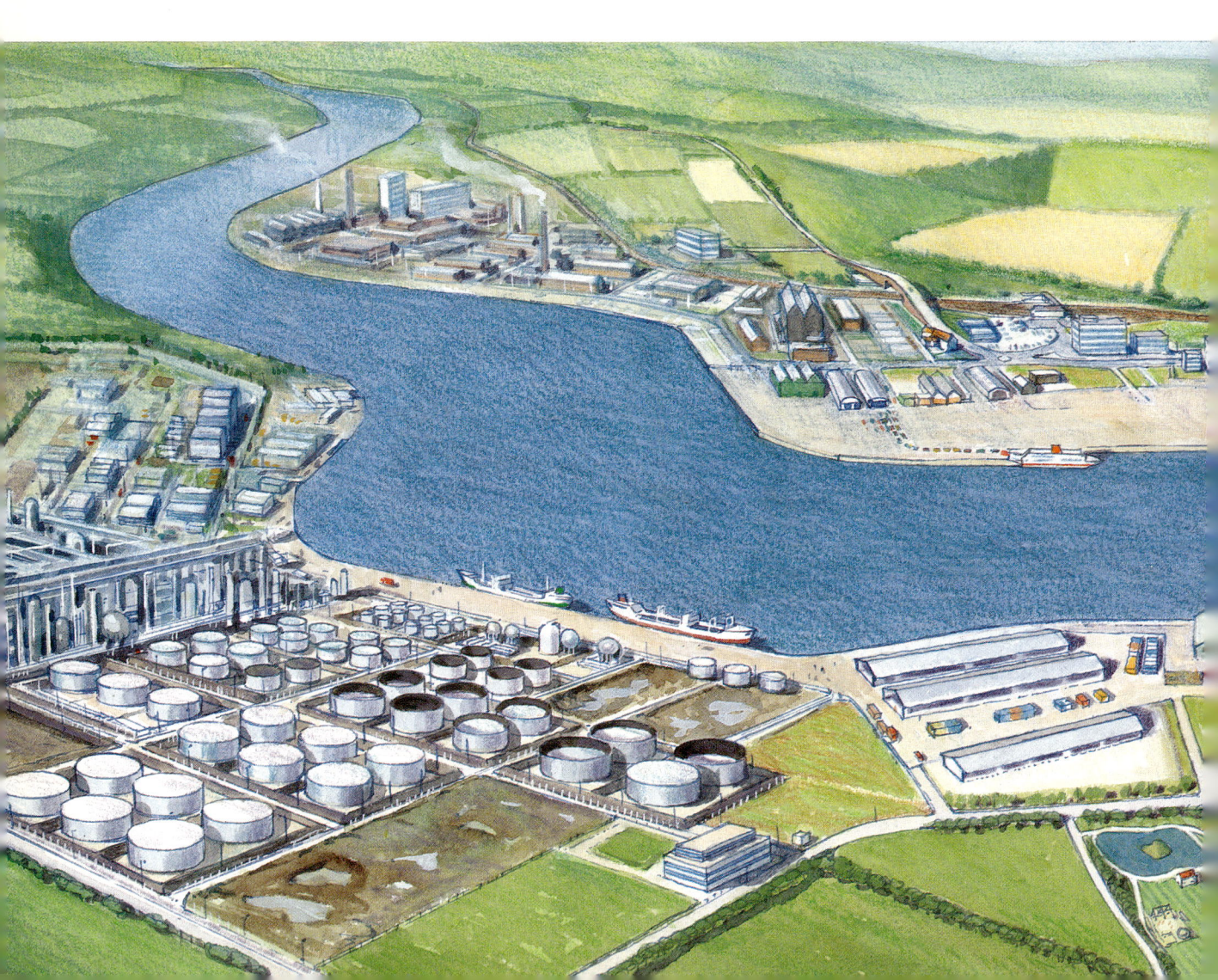

It is a port.
Ships from other places come to the port.
They bring goods and take goods away.
People also travel to and from the port.

People travel over the sea to other countries in other parts of the world.
Places in different parts of the world are different from each other.

Some places are hot. Some are cold.
They have different climates.
Around the middle of the world it is hot.
At the top and bottom it is icy cold.
In between, the climate is in between.

14

15

Some places are better than others to live in.
The weather is not too hot or cold.
The land is good for farming and there is rain.
People have lots of food to eat.

Some places are not so good to live in.
They are too hot, too dry or too cold.
The land is poor and it is hard to grow crops.
The people have little to eat.

Most people live crowded together in places where crops will grow.
Many live where there is rain or where they can get water from rivers.
Many live in cities where they can get work.

polar regions

deserts

tropical forests

mountains

Very few people live in these places.
Can you think why?

What kind of place do you live in?
Can you describe your home and your country?
Is it like this?
What is the climate like?
What is the countryside like?

More about the world

Where we live
The world is our home. Geography is the study of our world. It is good to know all about it. You need to know where your home is, which country it is in, and what the land you live in is like. Then you can find out out about all the places in the world.

Maps
When you want to know where something is you can look at a map. A map shows where towns, roads, rivers, mountains, lakes and other things can be found. Some maps show how high mountains are and even how deep the sea is in different places.

What places are like
As well as looking at maps, you can also look at pictures that show what a place is like and read books about it. You can see whether there are forests and lakes or fields and farms. You can see what kind of animals and plants live in an area or used to live there once. You can find out how people have changed a place by cutting down trees or building cities. You can work out what can be done to keep places clean and beautiful.

Climate
The diagram on page 15 shows what climates are generally like in different parts of the world. But many things affect climate. Being near or far from the sea makes a difference to climate and so does the height of the land. It gets colder and colder as you go up a mountain. In parts of Africa, where it is very hot on low land, you can see snow on the tops of the mountains.

Where people live
A good climate for farming is one with the right amount of sunshine and the right amount of rain. Farmers also need fertile (good) soil. Life is easier for people who live in areas where crops grow easily. The land by rivers is usually fertile, so river valleys are often crowded. Many people live in towns or cities where they can get work.

1

1 Where do you live? Do you live in a house or a flat?

2 Do you live in a town or in the country?

3 What do farmers use fields for?

4 Which is bigger, a town or a village?

5 Draw a picture of where you live.

6 What can you see in this picture?

2

7 Where does a river flow to? Where does it flow from?

8 Is the countryside crowded?

9 How far do you travel to school each day? How long does it take?

10 Why do few people live in hilly places?

11 Why are airports built near towns?

12 What is the name for a town that is visited by ships?

13 Where are the coldest parts of the world? Where are the hottest?

14 Can you find the place where you live on a map?

15 What is the climate like where you live? Is it different in summer and winter?

3

16 Make a geography notebook. Write in it the answers to these questions and any questions that you think of. Draw pictures and maps in it.

17 Why do few people live in deserts? Why do few people live in very cold places?

18 What kind of climate is best for farming? What kind of soil is best?

19 What kind of crops do farmers grow where you live?

20 Draw a map of your classroom. Show where the teacher sits and where the chairs and tables are. Show the doors and windows.

21 Draw a map of your home. Make it big enough to show where your school is. Show other important places as well. Is there a river?

22 Why do people move from the countryside into the towns?

23 Once there were lots and lots of forests in the world. Many have been cut down. Can you think why?

24 What do people use timber from cut-down trees for? What do they use land cleared of trees for?

25 Find out how old the place where you live is. What was there before people built their homes there?

26 What country do you live in? Find out how many people live in your country.

27 What is a continent? Which continent is your country in?

Index

airport 5, 22
animals 7, 21
books 21
bridges 4
building 6, 8
buses 5
cars 5
cities 18, 21
classroom 23
cleared land 23
climate 14, 15, 20, 21, 22, 23
coast 12
cold places 14, 15, 16, 17, 21, 22, 23
continent 23
country 14, 20, 21, 23
countryside 6, 7, 8, 20, 22, 23
crops 7, 17, 18, 21, 23
crowded places 4, 18, 22
depth of sea 21
deserts 19, 23
different places 14, 16, 17
dry places 17
eating 16, 17
farmers 7, 22, 23
farming 10, 16, 21, 23
farms 7, 8, 21

fertile soil 21
few people 19, 23
fields 6, 7, 10, 21, 22
flat 3, 22
food 7, 16, 17
forest 10, 21, 23
geography 21, 23
goods 13
height of land 21
hills 10, 11, 12, 22
homes 9, 20, 21, 23
hot places 14, 15, 16, 17, 22
houses 3, 22
how many people 23
lakes 21
land 16, 21
many people 18
map 6, 21, 22, 23
mountains 19, 21
offices 4
people 3, 4, 8, 10, 13, 17, 18
pictures 21, 22, 23
places 21
plants 21
polar regions 19
poor land 17
port 13
questions 22, 23
railway 6
rain 16, 18

river 4, 6, 11, 12, 18, 21, 22, 23
roads 5, 21
school 9, 23
sea 12, 14, 21
ships 13, 22
shops 4
snow 21
soil 21, 23
station 5
summer 22
sunshine 21
timber 23
town 3, 6, 8, 11, 12, 21, 22, 23
travel 9, 13, 14, 22
trees 10, 21
tropical forests 19
villages 8, 22
water 18
weather 16
where you live 20, 22
winter 22
work 18, 22
world 14, 21